INDIGENOUS LEGENDS 2

EXTRAORDINARY NATIVES

1491
PUBLISHING

INDIGENOUS LEGENDS 2
EXTRAORDINARY NATIVES

WRITTEN
AND
ILLUSTRATED BY
HENRY "CLOUD" ANDRADE

1491 PUBLISHING

INDIGENOUS LEGENDS 2
EXTRAORDINARY NATIVES

WRITTEN AND ILLUSTRATED BY
HENRY "CLOUD" ANDRADE

GRAPHICS AND DESIGN BY
OMAR "PANDA" ORNELAS CERVANTES

COVER ART BY
HENRY "CLOUD" ANDRADE

EDITED BY
ISHMEL MEHSI PINEIRO

PUBLISHED BY 1491 PUBLISHING
1491PUBLISHING@GMAIL.COM

COPYRIGHT ©1491 LLC
ISBN-13: 978-1-948698-02-3
ISBN-10: 1-948698-02-1

AVAILABLE ON 1491PUBLISHING.COM
AMAZON.COM AND OTHER RETAIL OUTLETS.

PRINTED IN OCCUPIED TURTLE ISLAND
(CURRENTLY KNOWN AS THE UNITED STATES OF AMERICA).

1491
PUBLISHING

INDIGENOUS LEGENDS
OUR WOMEN, OUR LEADERS

SHARICE Davids

SHARICE DAVIDS
(HO-CHUNK NATION)
FIRST NATIVE AMERICAN ELECTED TO
CONGRESSWOMAN ALONGSIDE
DEB HAALAND.
SHARICE IS AN MMA FIGHTER AND IS
ALSO THE FIRST LGBT IN CONGRESS.

DEB Haaland

DEB HAALAND
(LAGUNA PUEBLO)
FIRST NATIVE AMERICAN
IN CONGRESS,
ALONGSIDE SHARICE DAVIDS.

@SHARICEDAVIDS

@DEB4CONGRESSNM

ORENE Askew

ORENE ASKEW
AKA DJ OSHOW (SQUAMISH NATION)
COMMUNITY LEADER FROM
VANCOUVER BC AND PROUD
2 SPIRITED SPOKESPERSON FOR
THE SQUAMISH NATION COUNCIL.

PEGGY Flanagan

PEGGY FLANAGAN
(WHITE EARTH OJIBWA)
LIEUTENANT GOVERNOR OF MINNESOTA
AND FIRST NATIVE WOMAN
TO ADDRESS THE DEMOCRATIC NATIONAL
CONVENTION FROM THE PODIUM.

@DJSHOW

@PEGGYFLANAGAN

17

INDIGENOUS LEGENDS
THE BIG SCREEN AND TV

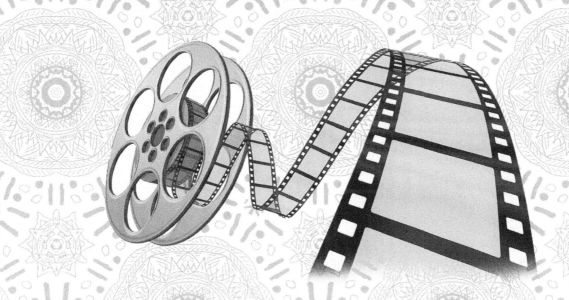

19

SAGINAW
Grant

SAGINAW GRANT
(SAC N FOX NATION)
HEREDITARY CHIEF OF THE
SAC AND FOX NATION
AND ACTOR KNOWN FOR HIS WORK
IN FILMS SUCH AS
'THE LONE RANGER'
AND 'THE RIDICULOUS 6'.

21

@SAGINAWGRANT

@YALITZAAPARICIO

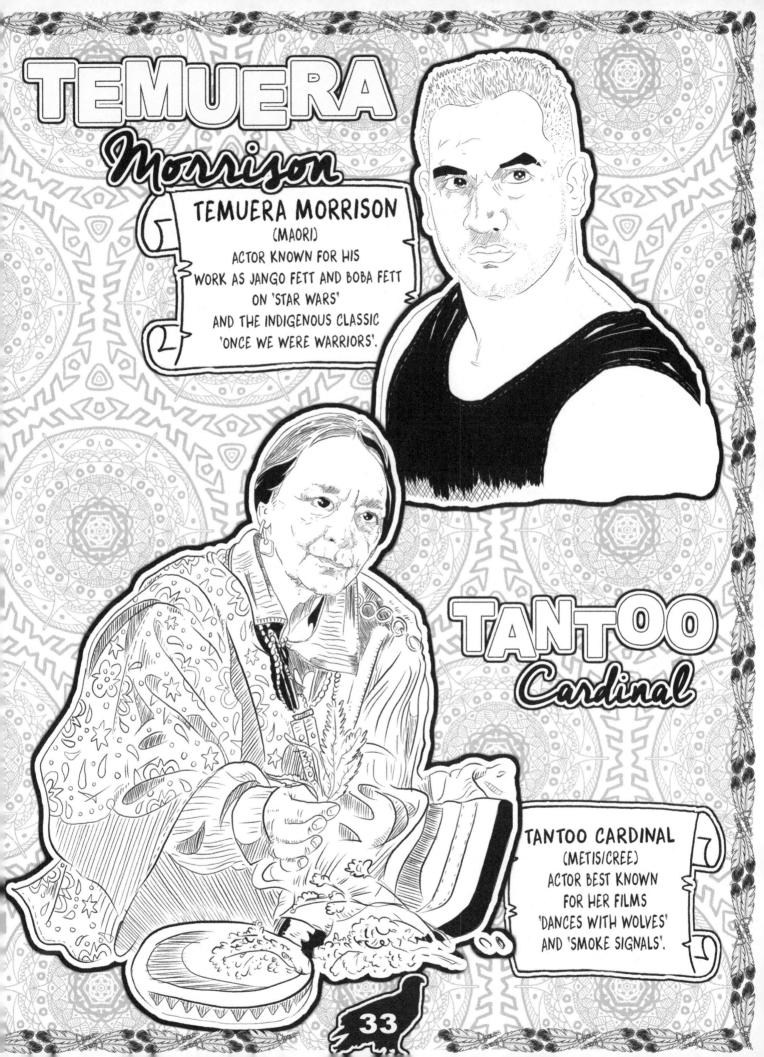

TEMUERA Morrison

TEMUERA MORRISON
(MAORI)
ACTOR KNOWN FOR HIS
WORK AS JANGO FETT AND BOBA FETT
ON "STAR WARS"
AND THE INDIGENOUS CLASSIC
"ONCE WE WERE WARRIORS".

TANTOO Cardinal

TANTOO CARDINAL
(METIS/CREE)
ACTOR BEST KNOWN
FOR HER FILMS
"DANCES WITH WOLVES"
AND "SMOKE SIGNALS".

@TEM_MORRISON
@TEMUERAMORRISON

@TANTOOC

GIL Birmingham

GIL BIRMINGHAM
(COMANCHE)
ACTOR BEST KNOWN
FOR HIS ROLE AS BILLY BLACK
ON 'THE TWILIGHT SAGA' AND
CHIEF RAINWATER ON
, 'YELLOWSTONE'.

GRACE Dove

GRACE DOVE
(SHUSWAP)
ACTOR BEST KNOWN FOR HER
WORK ON THE FILM
"THE REVENANT" AND
"ALASKA DAILY".

37

@GILBIRMINGHAM

@_GRACEDOVE

INDIGENOUS LEGENDS
NATIVE HIP HOP AND R&B

DJ Shub

DJ SHUB
(MOHAWK)
FORMERLY OF A 'TRIBE CALLED RED',
JUNO AWARD WINNING
DJ AND PRODUCER.
(PICTURED WITH CLASSIC ROOTS).

@DJSHUB

@CLASSICROOTS
@OFFICIALCLASSICROOTS
@CLASSIC_ROOTS

SNOTTY NOSE
Rez Kids

SNOTTY NOSE REZ KIDS
(HAISLA FIRST NATIONS)

JUNO NOMINATED,
CANADIAN HIP HOP GROUP.

LIL Mike & FUNNY Bone

LIL MIKE AND FUNNY BONE
(PAWNEE)
HIP HOP RECORDING ARTISTS
BEST KNOWN
FOR THEIR PHENOMENAL
PERFORMANCE
ON AMERICAS GOT TALENT.

@SNOTTYNOSEREZKIDS
@DJKOOKUM
@DEEJAYKOOKUM

@MIKEBONEMUSIC

ARTSON

ARTSON

(TARAHUMARA)

HIP HOP RECORDING ARTIST, BBOY, NAMMY AWARD WINNER FOR HIS ALBUM, "BRAVESTAR" AND CAST MEMEBER OF BEAR GREASE MUSICAL

NIGHT SHIELD

NIGHT SHIELD

(ROSEBUD LAKOTA) NAMMY AWARD WINNING RAPPER AND HOST OF SIOUX EMPIRE PODCAST.

@IAMARSTON

@NIGHTSHIELD

OLMECA

OLMECA
(TEPEHUANE)
HIP HOP ARTIST,
ACTIVIST AND
MEMBER OF INFLUENTIAL
HIP HOP GROUP, 'ACID REIGN'.

PJ Vegas

PJ VEGAS
(YAQUI)
R&B SINGER
AND MEMBER OF THE
MTV AWARD WINNING GROUP,
'MAG 7'.

55

@OLMECAOFFICIAL

@THEREALPJVEGAS

INDIGENOUS LEGENDS
BBOY MOUNT RUSHMORE

MR. WIGGLES
(TAINO)
MEMBER OF
ROCK STEADY
CREW/ELECTRIC
BOOGALOOS

REMIND
(LAKOTA)
MEMBER OF
STYLE
ELEMENTS/WEAPONS
OF MASS EXPRESSION

RANDY BOOGIE
(NAVAJO)
MEMBER OF
FOUNDATIONS
OF FREEDOM

BBOY THESIS
(YAQUI)
MEMBER OF
KNUCKLEHEADS
CALI/FRESH
DESCENDANTS

@MRWIGGLESRSC

@BSTARREMIND1977

@RANDY_BOOGIE

@BBOYTHESIS

INDIGENOUS LEGENDS
RATTLE AND DRUM

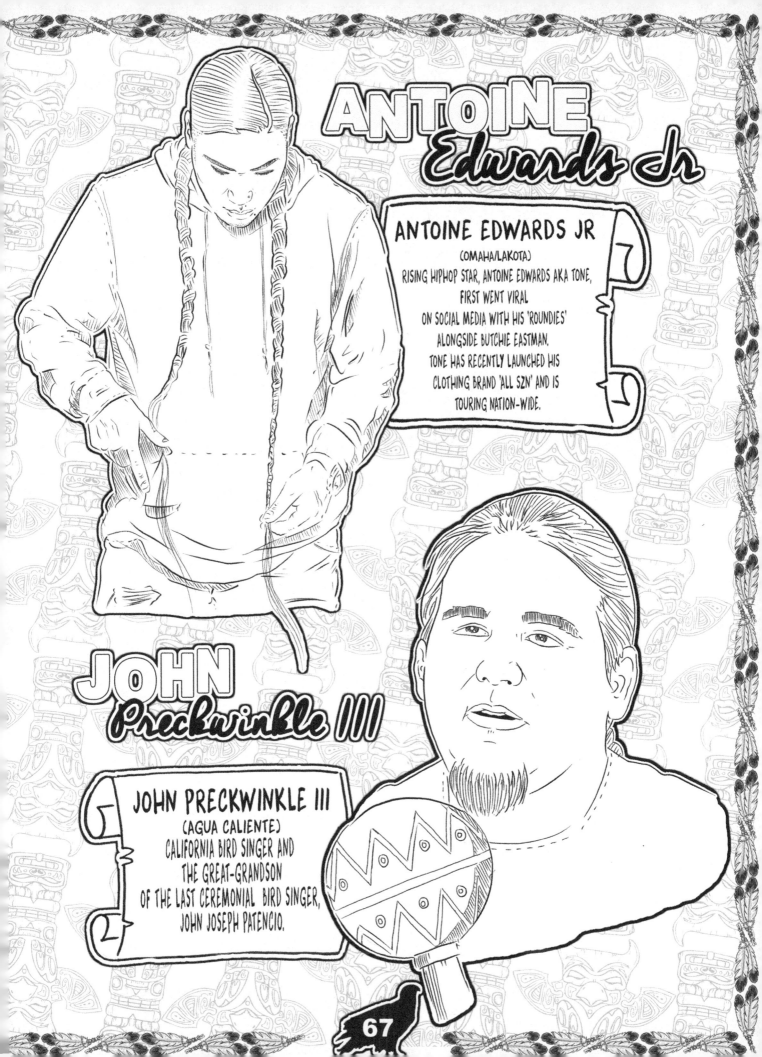

ANTOINE Edwards Jr

ANTOINE EDWARDS JR
(OMAHA/LAKOTA)
RISING HIPHOP STAR, ANTOINE EDWARDS AKA TONE,
FIRST WENT VIRAL
ON SOCIAL MEDIA WITH HIS 'ROUNDIES'
ALONGSIDE BUTCHIE EASTMAN.
TONE HAS RECENTLY LAUNCHED HIS
CLOTHING BRAND 'ALL SZN' AND IS
TOURING NATION-WIDE.

JOHN Preckwinkle III

JOHN PRECKWINKLE III
(AGUA CALIENTE)
CALIFORNIA BIRD SINGER AND
THE GREAT-GRANDSON
OF THE LAST CEREMONIAL BIRD SINGER,
JOHN JOSEPH PATENCIO.

@ANTOINE.E.JR
@ANTOINEEDWARDS.JR

@NATIVEFROMCALI

MIDNITE Express

MIDNITE EXPRESS
(OJIBWE, MENOMINEE, LAKOTA, HOCHUNK AND PUEBLO)
THE MNX SINGERS ARE A CHAMPION DRUM GROUP FROM
THE TWIN CITIES. THEY HAVE WON SEVERAL GATHERING OF
NATIONS COMPETITIONS AND NAMMY AWARDS
FOR THEIR POW WOW RECORDINGS.

@MNXSINGERS

INDIGENOUS LEGENDS
SPORTS

KENNY *Dobbs*

KENNY DOBBS
(CHOCTAW NATION)
SLAM DUNK CHAMPION OF THE WORLD.
KENNY'S VERTICAL JUMP TRAINING
AND DUNK ARTISTRY
HAVE BEEN SEEN ON
NBA TV, ESPN AND FOX SPORTS.

LEVI *Horn*

LEVI HORN
(CHEYENNE)
FORMER AMERICAN
FOOTBALL OFFENSIVE TACKLE,
ALL BIG-SKY CONFERENCE
PLAYER, AND AN
FCS ALL AMERICAN WHO
PLAYED FOR THE
CHICAGO BEARS AND
MINNESOTA VIKINGS.

KYRIE *Irving*

KYRIE IRVING
(STANDING ROCK)
#11 GUARD FOR DALLAS MAVERICKS;
2016 OLYMPIAN GOLD MEDALIST,
6X NBA ALL STAR MVP, AND
NBA CHAMPION.

@THEKENNYDOBBS

@LEVIHORN

@KYRIEIRVING

MARIA LORENA *Ramirez*

MARIA LORENA RAMIREZ
(TARAHUMARA)
A RARAMURI RUNNER;
ULTRA-MARATHON CHAMPION
OF THE ULTRA
TRAIL CERRO ROJO.

JoRDAN *Nolan*

JORDAN NOLAN
(OJIBWE/MALISEET)
HAS WON 2 STANLEY CUPS
WITH THE
LOS ANGELES KINGS.

INDIGENOUS LEGENDS
DANCE ME OUTSIDE

ACOSIA
Red Elk

ACOSIA RED ELK
(UMITILLA NATION)
10X GATHERING OF
NATIONS WORLD CHAMPION
JINGLE DRESS DANCER
AND CREATOR OF
POW WOW YOGA.

@ACOSIAREDELK
@ACOSIAELK
@ACOSIA_

SEAN Snyder

ADRIAN
Matthias-Stevens

SEAN SNYDER
(NAVAJO/SOUTHERN UTE)

ADRIAN MATTHIAS-STEVENS
(SHOSHONE/BANNOCK/UTE/APACHE)
POW WOW
CHAMPIONS FAMOUS FOR
BEING THE FIRST
2 SPIRIT COUPLE TO
WIN THE
'SWEETHEARTS DANCE'.

91

@ADSTEVENS

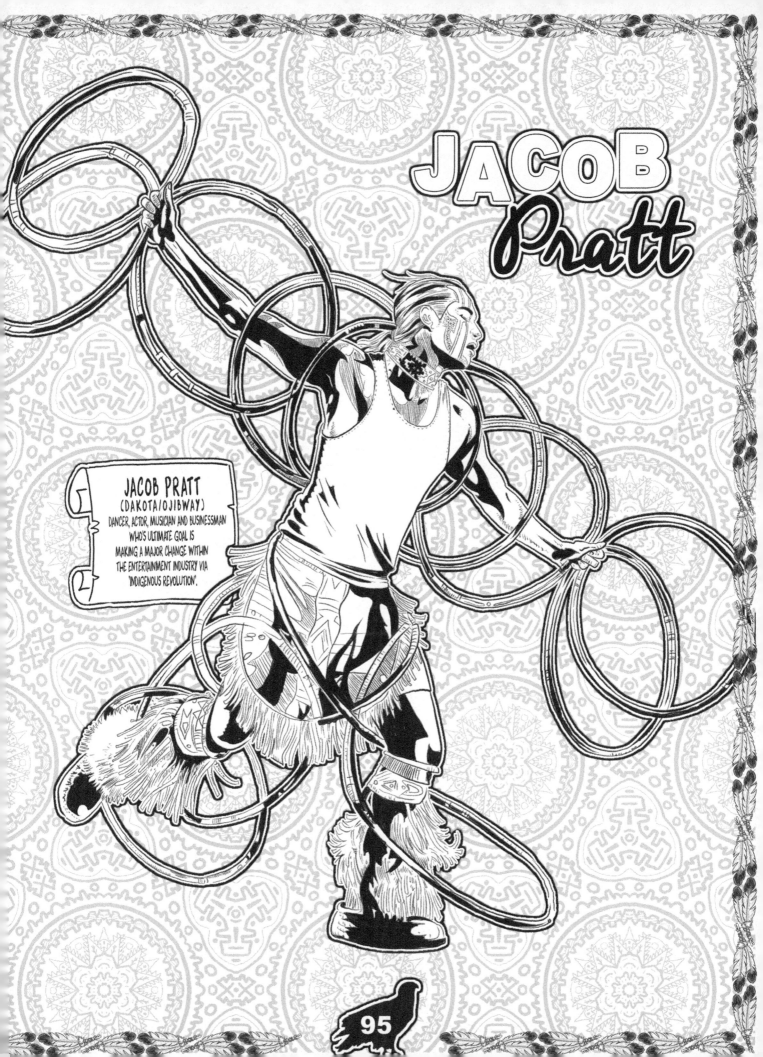

JACOB Pratt

JACOB PRATT
(DAKOTA/OJIBWAY)
DANCER, ACTOR, MUSICIAN AND BUSINESSMAN
WHO'S ULTIMATE GOAL IS
MAKING A MAJOR CHANGE WITHIN
THE ENTERTAINMENT INDUSTRY VIA
'INDIGENOUS REVOLUTION'.

@JAKE.DAKOTA
@JAKE_DAKOTA
@JACOBPRATT

ANGELA MIRACLE
Gladue

ANGELA MIRACLE GLADUE
(CREE)
CHOREOGRAPHER AND DANCER FOR
JUNO AWARD WINNERS: A TRIBE CALLED RED

@MISSCHIEFROCKA

INDIGENOUS LEGENDS
NATIVE FOLK, COUNTRY AND ROCK

KLEE Benally

KLEE BENALLY
(NAVAJO)
INDIGENOUS ACTIVIST
AND
SINGER/MUSICIAN
FOR 'BLACKFIRE'.

PETE Sands

PETE SANDS
(NAVAJO)
SINGER, ACTOR, AND WRITER KNOWN
FOR HIS WORK ON
PARAMOUNT NETWORK'S 'YELLOWSTONE'.

105

@KLEEBENALLY
@EELK

@SANDSPETE
@PETESANDSMAN

QUETZAL *Guerrero*

QUETZAL GUERRERO
(MEXIKA/BRASIL)
QVLN IS A CLASSICALLY TRAINED
VIOLINIST, SINGER, MODEL,
DANCER AND CAPOEIRISTA,
NOW RESIDING IN NEW ZEALAND.

INDIAN *City*

INDIAN CITY
(FIRST NATIONS)
FOUNDED BY AWARD WINNING
SINGER VINCE FONTAINE OF
EAGLE AND HAWK,
"INDIAN CITY" IS A JUNO NOMINATED
FOLK ROCK
BAND FROM
CANADA.

@QVIOLIN

@INDIANCITYMUSIC

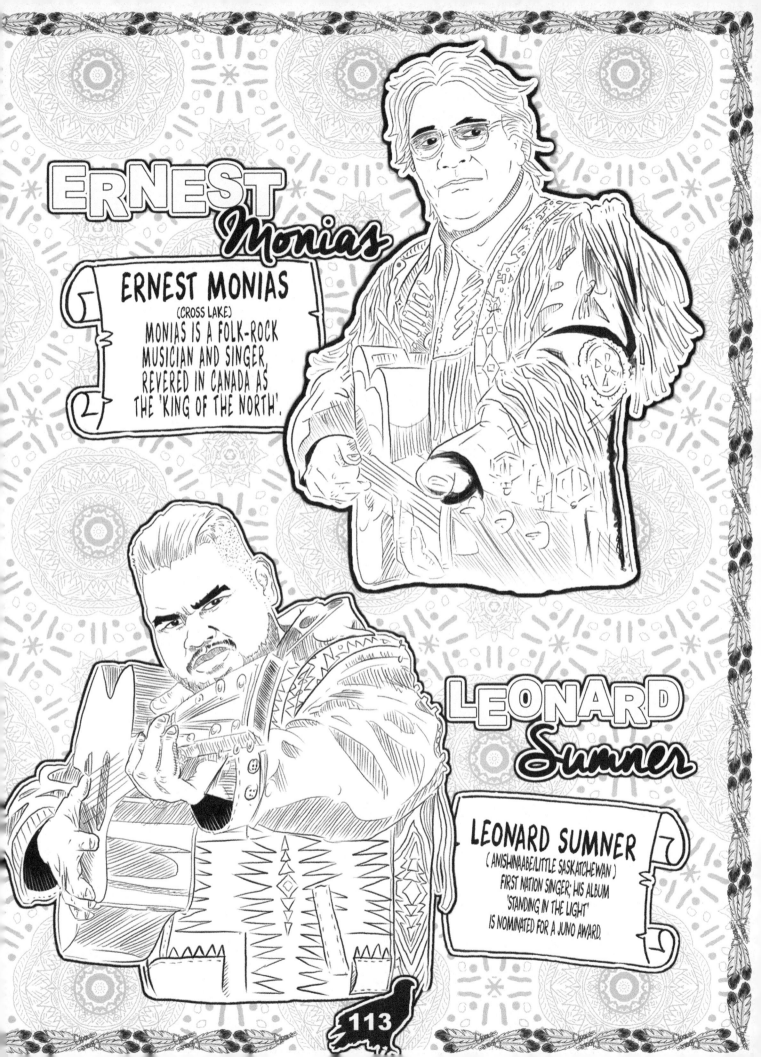

ERNEST Monias

ERNEST MONIAS
(CROSS LAKE)
MONIAS IS A FOLK-ROCK MUSICIAN AND SINGER, REVERED IN CANADA AS THE 'KING OF THE NORTH'.

LEONARD Sumner

LEONARD SUMNER
(ANISHINAABE/LITTLE SASKATCHEWAN)
FIRST NATION SINGER; HIS ALBUM 'STANDING IN THE LIGHT' IS NOMINATED FOR A JUNO AWARD.

113

@ERNESTMONIAS

@LEONARDSUMNER

KEITH Secola

KEITH SECOLA

(ANISHINAABE)
SINGER/MUSICIAN OF
"KEITH SECOLA
AND THE BAND OF WILD INDIANS".
KNOWN FOR HIS
NATIVE CULT-CLASSIC SONG
'NDN CARS'.
IN 2016, SECOLA WAS INDUCTED
INTO THE NATIVE AMERICAN
MUSIC AWARDS
HALL OF FAME.

@KEITHSCOLA

INDIGENOUS LEGENDS
LEAGUES OF THEIR OWN

RICHARD
Wagamese

RICHARD WAGAMESE
(OJIBWE)
AUTHOR OF BEST SELLING NOVEL
"INDIAN HORSE";
BURT AWARD WINNER FOR
FIRST NATIONS LITERATURE.

@RICHARDWAGAMESE

BIRD Runningwater

BIRD RUNNINGWATER
(CHEYENNE AND MESCALERO APACHE)
PROGRAMMER OF NATIVE INITIATIVES AT THE SUNDANCE INSTITUTE, RUNNINGWATER HELPS INDIGENOUS FILMMAKERS GET WORLDWIDE ATTENTION FOR THEIR PROJECTS.

TANAYA Winder

TANAYA WINDER
(DUCKWATER SHOSHONE)
POET, WRITER, ARTIST AND EDUCATOR.
FOUNDER OF 'DREAM WARRIORS'
AND CO FOUNDER OF 'AS/US:
A SPACE FOR WOMEN OF THE WORLD'.

@IZHASHE
@BIRDRUNNINGH2O

@TANAYAWINDER

SUZETTE Amaya

SUZETTE AMAYA
(GWASALA NAKWAXDAXW NATION)
FOUNDER OF
THINK NDN RADIO
AND CAST OF
BIG BROTHER CA.

LEONARD Peltier

LEONARD PELTIER

(LAKOTA/DAKOTA/CHIPPEWA)
MEMBER OF THE
AMERICAN INDIAN MOVEMENT.
PELTIER IS SERVING A
LIFE SENTENCE FOR
THE DEATH OF 2 FBI AGENTS.
AMNESTY INTERNATIONAL
CLAIMS THAT PELTIER IS A
POLITICAL PRISONER
WHO SHOULD BE
IMMEDIATELY RELEASED.

@SUZETTEAMAYA

WRITE YOUR CONGRESSMAN

HTTPS://WWW.HOUSE.GOV/REPRESENTATIVES/FIND-YOUR-REPRESENTATIVE

SEND CARDS AND LETTERS

LEONARD PELTIER

#89637-132 USPCOLEMAN I

U.S. PENITENTIARY

P.O. BOX 1033 COLEMAN, FL 33521

INDIGENOUS LEGENDS
THE ARTISTS WILL AWAKEN THE PEOPLE

NORVAL Morrisseau

NORVAL MORRISSEAU
(OJIBWE)
WIDELY REGARDED AS THE GRANDFATHER
OF CONTEMPORARY
INDIGENOUS ART IN CANADA.

@OFFICIALNORVALMORRISSEAU
@NORVALMOFFICIAL

JoHN IsAiAH Pepion

JOHN ISAIAH PEPION
(BLACKFOOT)
WORLD RENOWN
LEDGER ARTIST
FROM MONTANA.

LoUiE Gong

LOUIE GONG
(NOOKSACK)
ARTIST, EDUCATOR,
PUBLIC SPEAKER
AND FOUNDER
OF 8TH GENERATION.
BEST KNOWN FOR
HIS HIGHLY SOUGHT
AFTER, CUSTOM MADE SHOES
AND FIRST OF ITS KIND,
NATIVE OWNED
WOOL BLANKETS.

@JOHNISAIAHEPION

@8THGEN
@EIGTH_GENERATION

CILAU Valadez

CILAU VALADEZ
(WIXARIKA)
WIXARIKA YARN PAINTER AND SON OF
RENOWN MASTER ARTISAN MARIANO VALADEZ

@CILAU.VALADEZ

NANI Chacon

NANI CHACON
(DINE'/XICANA)
MURALIST ARTIST BEST KNOWN FOR HER LOUD AND PROUD USE OF INDIGENOUS WOMEN IN BRIGHT AND BOLD COLORS. NANI USES HER ART TO PLACE A SPOTLIGHT ON THE INJUSTICES BEING BROUGHT ON BROWN WOMEN.

STEPHANIE Big Eagle

STEPHANIE BIG EAGLE
(DAKOTA)
SINGER, WATER PROTECTOR AND TATTOO ARTIST BEHIND THE STANDING ROCK DESIGN. BIG EAGLE IS ALSO A TRADITIONAL AND CONTEMPORARY DANCER.

@NANI.CHACONI
@NANIBAH

@STEPHBIGEAGLE

CODY Sanderson

CODY SANDERSON

(NAVAJO)

DENE' SILVERSMITH WITH A WILD IMAGINATION
FOR JEWELRY. SANDERSON'S INNOVATIVE DESIGNS HAVE
EARNED HIM NUMEROUS AWARDS INCLUDING
THE PRESTIGIOUS "BEST IN SHOW" AT THE HEARD MUSEUM.

@CODYSANDDESIGNS
@CODYSANDERSONDESIGNS

INDIGENOUS LEGENDS
HEALTH AND WELLNESS

THOSH Collins

THOSH COLLINS

(SALT RIVER O'ODHAM)

ADVOCATE FOR NATIVE HEALTH AND CO-FOUNDER OF THE "WELL FOR CULTURE" INDIGENOUS WELLNESS INITIATIVE.

DEB Echohawk

DEB ECHOHAWK

(PAWNEE NATION)

KEEPER OF THE SEEDS FOR THE PAWNEE NATION OF OKLAHOMA SEED PRESERVATION PROJECT.

@THOSH.COLLINS

@DEBECHOHAWKDEB

INDIGENOUS LEGENDS
CHEFS

DANIELA
Soto-Innes

DANIELA SOTO - INNES
(MEXIKA)
NATIVE OF MEXICO CITY,
NAMED
"WORLDS BEST FEMALE CHEF"
IN 2019. DANIELA'S
SIGNATURE DISHES
CAN BE FOUND IN
NEW YORK CITY'S "COSME".

RICH
Francis

RICH FRANCIS
(SIX NATIONS)
"MASTER OF MODERN INDIGENOUS CUISINE"
AND FINALIST ON CANADA'S TOP CHEF.

@DANIELASOTOINES

@7THFIRE
@GWICHINTRIBAL

SHANE Chartrand

SHANE CHARTRAND
(SIX NATIONS)
(ENOCH CREE)
FINALIST ON CHOPPED CANADA AND AUTHOR
OF INDIGENOUS COOKBOOK 'TAWAW'.
SHANES SIGNATURE DISHES
CAN BE FOUND AT 'DAMN GOOD FOOD'
IN EDMONTON'S RIVER CREE CASINO.

@CHEFSHANECHARTRAND
@SHANEMCHARTRAND
@CHEFCHARTRAND

INDIGENOUS LEGENDS
MODELS AND THE FASHION WORLD

CHASE *Manhattan*

CHASE MANHATTAN
(LAKOTA, MUSCOGEE, OJIBWE)
HIP HOP RECORDING ARTIST
AND FOUNDER OF HUSTLE TRIBE CLOTHING.

JARED *Yazzie*

JARED YAZZIE
(NAVAJO)
FASHION DESIGNER, FOUNDER AND
ARTIST BEHIND THE NATIVE
OWNED BRAND: OXDX.

TODD *Harder*

TODD HARDER
(NIBWAAKAAWIN)
CEO OF NATIVE SKATES. TODD PARTNERED
WITH VANS FOR
THE POPULAR 'PENDLETON BLANKET VANS'.
FOUNDER OF THE
ALL NATIONS NATIVE SKATE JAM.

@HUSTLETRIBE

@OXDXCLOTHING

@ALLNATIONSSKATE

@THEBAKERTWINS

KELLY Holmes

KELLY HOLMES
(CHEYENNE RIVER LAKOTA)
MODEL AND CEO OF NATIVE MAX MAGAZINE

MARIAH Watchman

MARIAH WATCHMAN
(UMATILLA/MANDAN)
INTERNATIONAL MODEL SINCE
THE AGE OF 15 AND FIRST NATIVE AMERICAN TO
APPEAR ON
AMERICAS NEXT TOP MODEL.

LINSAY Willier

LINSAY WILLIER
(WOODLANDS CREE/SUCKER CREEK)
FIRST NATIONS MODEL KNOWN FOR HER
WORK ON CANADAS NEXT TOP MODEL.
LINSAY HAS HER BACHELORS IN
CHILD DEVELOPMENT AND HAS WON
THE PEOPLES CHOICE AWARD FOR
MISS UNIVERSE CANADA.

@KELLZHOLMES

@MARIAHWATCHMAN

@LINSAYWILLIER

185

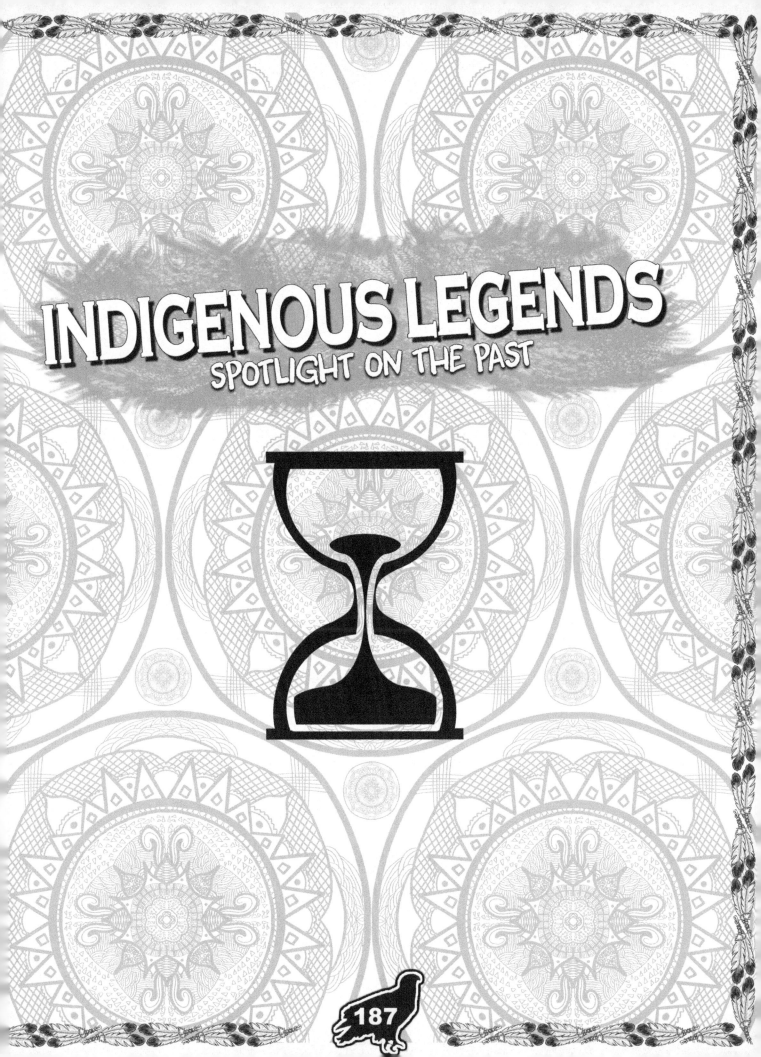

INDIGENOUS LEGENDS
SPOTLIGHT ON THE PAST

ELIZABETH Peratrovich

ELIZABETH PERATROVICH

(TLINGIT NATION)

CIVIL RIGHTS ACTIVIST WHO WORKED ON BEHALF OF EQUALITY FOR ALASKAN NATIVES. CREDITED WITH ADVOCACY THAT LEAD TO THE FIRST ANTI-DISCRIMINATION LAW OF THE UNITED STATES.

LOZEN

LOZEN

(CHIRACAHUA APACHE)

SKILLED MILITARY STRATEGIST, MEDICINE WOMAN AND SISTER OF VICTORIO. LOZEN WAS A PROPHET OF THE CHIHENNE AND ACCORDING TO LEGENDS, WAS ABLE TO USE HER POWERS IN BATTLE AND LEARN ENEMY MOVEMENTS.

INDIGENOUS LEGENDS
SPOTLIGHT ON THE FUTURE

SHALENE Joseph

SHALENE JOSEPH
(A'ANIII, ATHABASCAN)
MASTERS AT UCLA AMERICAN INDIAN STUDIES,
SHALENE HAS RECENTLY CO-WRITTEN AND CO-DIRECTED
A SHORT FILM ON MENTAL HEALTH AND IS ALSO A CURRENT
AMBASSADOR AT 'INDIGENOUS 20 SOMETHING'S PROJECT'

SHYLA Latone

SHYLA LATONE
(ZUNI/PUEBLO)
HIGH SCHOOL GIRLS BASKETBALL
POINT GUARD. SHYLA WAS
NAMED CALIFORNIA
INTERSCHOLASTIC-FEDERATION AND
METRO LEAGUE PLAYER OF THE YEAR.

PHRASE Frazier

PHRASE FRAZIER
(NAVAJO)
SOUTHWEST BATTLE RAPPER
ON THE RISE.
PHRASE IS FOUNDER OF DAY ONES
AND ROOTED CLOTHING.

INDIGENOUS LEGENDS
COMEDY

THE 1491'S
(NATIVE SKETCH COMEDY GROUP)
MEMBERS INCLUDE: STERLIN HARJO,
RYAN REDCORN, DALLAS GOLDTOOTH,
BOBBY MARTIN AND MIGIZI PENSANEAU.

@1491s

TONIA JO Hall

TONIA JO HALL

(LAKOTA/DAKOTA/HIDATSA)
COMEDIAN KNOWN FOR
HER HILARIOUS PERSONA,
"AUNTIE BEACHRESS".
TONIA IS ALSO A MOTIVATIONAL
SPEAKER AND A
JINGLE DRESS DANCER.

MYLO Smith

MYLO SMITH

(CROW CREEK/DAKOTA)
COMEDIAN, EMCEE AND
MOTIVATIONAL SPEAKER
WHO ENJOYS
EATING FAST FOOD
WHILE WATCHING
STRANGERS WORK OUT.

@TONIAJOHALL

@MYLOSMITH

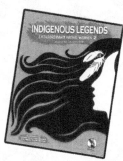

THE INDIGENOUS LEGENDS WORKSHOPS

BOOK THE WORKSHOP NOW!

HENRY "CLOUD" ANDRADE, (HUICHOL / WIXÁRIKA) IS AN AUTHOR, ILLUSTRATOR AND RECORDING ARTIST FROM HAWTHORNE, CA. HE IS A FORMER WORLD RECORD HOLDER FOR LONGEST FREESTYLE RAP AND A MEMBER OF POWER 106'S WINNING HIP-HOP GROUP, "LIGHTINGCLOUD." REDCLOUD'S FOCUS AND PASSION IS ACTIVISM THROUGH EDUCATION AND CREATIVE EXPRESSION. REDCLOUD IS ALSO THE WRITER AND CO CREATOR OF THE HIT MUSICAL "BEAR GREASE".

CRYSTLE LIGHTNING (ENOCH CREE NATION) IS AN ACTRESS, RECORDING ARTIST, DJ, AND CEO OF 1491 PUBLISHING. HER DEBUT RELEASE AS A PUBLISHER, "INDIGENOUS LEGENDS FROM A-Z COLORING BOOK," CAPTURED THE #1 SPOT FOR NEW RELEASES ON AMAZON. HER PERSEVERANCE, TENACITY AND CREATIVE ABILITIES ARE APPARENT IN HER CAREER AND SOCIAL JUSTICE WORK FOR MARGINALIZED COMMUNITIES.

INDIGENOUS LEGENDS WORKSHOP IS A COMBINATION OF MOTIVATIONAL SPEAKING+ MUSIC + ENTERTAINMENT SESSION TOPICS INCLUDE:

- CHASING YOUR DREAMS
- GANG ABATEMENT
- VISUAL ART THERAPY
- LANGUAGE REVITALIZATION THROUGH ART

- MUSIC + SONGWRITING
- ACTOR'S WORKSHOP
- FILMMAKING 101
- ART OF STORYTELLING

-MASTERCLASS EXPERIENCE

ALSO AVAILABLE FROM 1491 PUBLISHING

SCAN THE QR CODE FOR LINKS AND MORE INFO

BUY IT NOW AT amazon.com

INDEX

INDEX

Made in United States
Orlando, FL
27 June 2024